Seder in the Desert

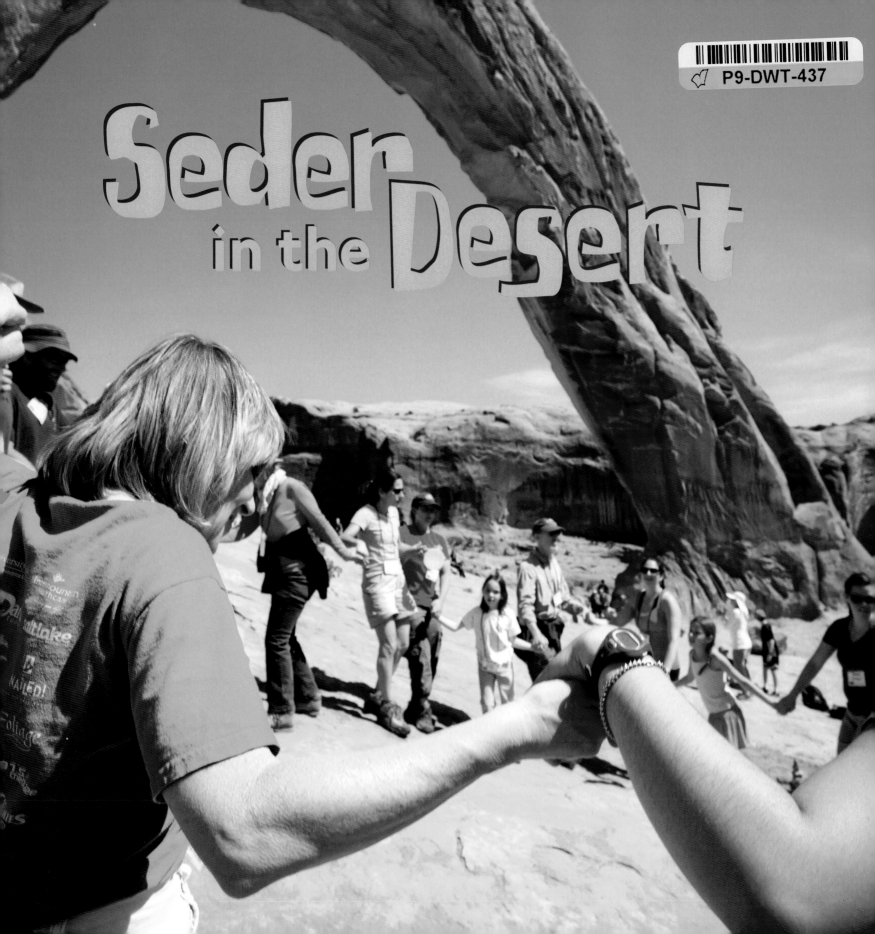

**To my favorite older sister,
K.T. Korngold
—J.K.**

**To my sister Lisa Ann
Finkelstein, I love sharing
Passover in the Desert with you.
—J.F.**

**To Ori – Too young to be
in these photos but a shining
light in our lives.
—J.K. and J.F.**

KAR-BEN PUBLISHING
A division of Lerner Publishing Group, Inc.
241 First Avenue North
Minneapolis, MN 55401 U.S.A.
1-800-4-KARBEN

Website address: www.karben.com

Main body text set in Johnston ITC Std Medium 16/25.
Typeface provided by International Typeface Corp.

Library of Congress Cataloging-in-Publication Data

Korngold, Jamie S.
Seder in the desert / by Jamie Korngold ;
illustrated by Jeff Finkelstein.
pages   cm
ISBN: 978-0-7613-7501-2 (lib. bdg. : alk. paper)
ISBN: 978-1-4677-2431-9 (eBook)
1. Passover—Juvenile literature. 2. Seder—Juvenile literature.
I. Finkelstein, Jeff illustrator. II. Title.
BM695.P3K67 2014
296.4'5371—dc23
2013002180

Manufactured in the United States of America
1 – MG – 12/31/13

Jamie Korngold   photos by Jeff Finkelstein

in the Desert

KAR-BEN
PUBLISHING

Why is this seder different from all others?

Because this year we are celebrating Passover in the desert.

Just like the Israelites, we are hiking. The walk is hard. We climb over red rocks, through sandy washes, and up slanted sandstone.

Rabbi Jamie tells us the Israelites had to help each other in order to survive. We help each other, too.

Our Torah is in a backpack. We carry it carefully while we hike.

The sun is hot, and I get thirsty. I spot a flower growing quietly in a crack. I wonder how it survives here with so little water. Now I understand how important water was for the Israelites.

Finally we arrive at the spot where we will have our seder. How different this is from our dining room at home! We spread out tablecloths on the ground and unpack our supplies.

We place the special foods on the seder plate.

We pass out the haggadahs. There is a special haggadah just for the kids.

We begin our seder. We ask the Four Questions and look for the answers as we tell the story of the Exodus.

We explain the symbols on the seder table.

With each crunch of our matzah, we remember that the Israelites did not have time to bake bread before they left Egypt. Instead, they put the raw dough on their backs, and the sun baked it into hard crackers.

The bone reminds us of the first time the Israelites celebrated Passover. They roasted a lamb and ate it with matzah.

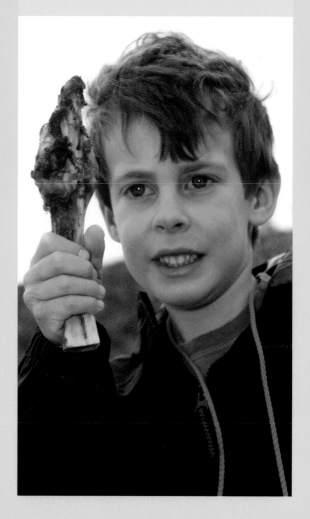

The egg reminds us of the birth of the Jewish nation and of new life that grows in the spring.

The parsley also reminds us of spring. One of the hardiest herbs of the garden, it also recalls how strong the Jewish people had to be to survive in the desert.

We open our backpack Torah and read the story of how Moses led the Israelite slaves from Egypt.

Like Miriam and the Israelite women, we sing "Dayenu" and dance with our tambourines. We have so much to be thankful for! God freed us from Egypt, split the sea, gave us the Torah, and brought us to the Promised Land.

It's time to eat. Because we all worked together, our seder meal tastes extra delicious. We remember that the Jewish people had to work together before they could become a nation.

We search for the afikomen. We cannot finish the seder without it.

Then we fill Miriam's and Elijah's cups.

Miriam's cup reminds us of the legendary well that followed Miriam and provided water for the Israelites as they wandered in the desert.

An ancient Jewish story tells us that Elijah the Prophet visits every seder to encourage us to work for peace and justice.

After we finish, we hike back
down the mountain.

Our celebration continues late into the night. After we recite Havdalah, we build a big campfire.

We sing songs beneath a full moon and hope
to celebrate Passover in the desert again.

About the Seder in the Desert

The Adventure Rabbi Passover Seder in Moab combines the ancient traditions of the Jewish seder with the inspiration of the Red Rock Desert. More than 250 people from over 18 states and five countries have joined the Adventure Rabbis, Rabbi Jamie Korngold and Rabbi Evon Yakar, on a unique Passover adventure, which reenacts the Israelites' exodus from Egypt. Together, the community hikes, learns, laughs, sings, debates, and of course enjoys delicious Passover foods. For more information about the Adventure Rabbi Program, visit www.AdventureRabbi.org.

Rabbi Jamie S. Korngold serves as the spiritual leader of the Adventure Rabbi Program. She received her ordination from Hebrew Union College-Jewish Institute of Religion. She has served as a congregational rabbi in the United States and Canada, a street musician in Japan, a cook on a boat in Alaska helping with the *Exxon Valdez* oil spill clean-up, and an Outward Bound guide. She is the author of *Sadie's Sukkah Breakfast*, *Sadie and the Big Mountain*, *Sadie's Almost Marvelous Menorah*, the best-selling *God in the Wilderness* (Doubleday) and *The God Upgrade* (Jewish Lights). She lives in Boulder, Colorado.

The Adventure Family in Moab: Rabbi Jamie Korngold , Sadie, Jeff Finkelstein, and Ori.

Jeff Finkelstein's images have graced the covers of books, magazines, and websites. A member of the National Press Photographers Association, he has images on permanent display in museums in three countries. His images have appeared in hundreds of publications. A former professional ski patrol, he is often seen skiing backwards down mogul runs at ski areas, camera in hand. He lives in Boulder, Colorado with his wife and two (well-photographed) daughters.